REFLECTIONS OF THE HEART

REFLECTIONS OF THE HEART

By

SHARON THORNE-MENSAH

SIMMS BOOKS PUBLISHING

SIMMS BOOKS PUBLISHING

Publishers Since 2012

Published By Simms Books Publishing

Jonesboro, GA

Library of Congress Cataloging in Publication Data

Sharon Thorne-Mensah

REFLECTIONS OF THE HEART

ISBN: 978-0-9983311-4-0

Printed in the United States of America

Book Arrangement by Simms Books Publishing

Edited by: Mary Hoekstra

Cover by Urias Brown, Michael Shield

DEDICATION

I dedicate this to my three beautiful children. Without them, I wouldn't be the woman I am today.

REFLECTIONS OF THE HEART

BONNIE AND CLYDE

Where did we go wrong?

It still seems to puzzle me.

We were Bonnie and Clyde.

I loved you and you loved me.

Now it seems as if the love has faded.

I still ponder the moments.

Seems like the waves have washed

away your feelings.

You seem so cold and distant and it's killing me inside.

All I needed was your love and to show me that I was

worth your time. I waited and waited and you thought it

was a joke. You assumed that I would be here forever; I

exited out of the game.

1

YESTERDAY

Yesterday, we were friends, now we're friends no more

because you walked out the door and your face hit the

floor. Now it's time for me to lock the door of my heart

because this poem is a metaphor.

YOU & I

You and I are meant to be together. Your smile, touch and

conversation gives me the shivers. I can't wait to be your

wife, so that I can be there for you morning, noon and

night.

WITH YOU

I just want to be your baby no one else will do.

I know I say I love you often

But every word I say is true.

You made me realize all men aren't the same.

I wrote your name in my heart and forever it will stay.

We have our ups and downs but no relationship is
perfect.

You've got my heart and you're the captain of my

emotions.

I love your smile, your eyes and your intelligence.

I thank God faithfully because it feels like you were
heaven

sent.

CONFUSED

I'm confused don't know what to do.

My heart is telling me one thing while my mind seems to

be drinking boozes.

I love you I do but what's a girl to do?

These feelings have got me singing the blues.

BRIANNA

On that cold January day

I awoke to make your bottle and see your beautiful face

Both something didn't feel right and I couldn't quite

figure

it out.

So I went to pick you up and you were cold to the touch.

My precious angel didn't make it through the night, why

God why was the words that came from my mouth.

You were only 3 months old what harm had you done?

Was I being punished for all the wrong I had done?

But Why God? Why take the most precious gift that

you

had given me and not allow me to witness the moments of

her growing up.

Everything happens for a reason. But I still have a hole

in

my heart and I'm giving it to YOU so that YOU can

make

it brand new.

WHY?

Why must you do this to me?

Sending mixed-signals is not my thing.

Keep it 100 and tell me how you feel,

This game you are playing is not a good deal.

HATE ME, LOVE ME

Hate me or Love me it doesn't make a difference.

I wasn't born to please you.

I was born to impact the nation.

NO MORE

What we had is no more and all because you saw me

literally like dirt on the floor. Two beautiful girls were the

fruit of your love.

I loved you with everything I had, even wanted to carry

your last name. But that wasn't the plan and now I can

see

clearly that you were just using me. So with that being

said;

I write you these words to thank you and I hope you find

love and that you can make it work.

SHE SAYS

She says; I want a marriage that is monogamous but she picked the guy she wanted and acted if God didn't exist...

God knew her before she was conceived, HIS plan for her life was written and ready to be retrieved but the cause of her actions have cost her much pain and the tears in her eyes seem like they will forever remain. She sits and looks at the tattoo on her wrist, the one with the name of the man she thought would love her forever and a day with no heartache just pure joy and bliss.

He says: My Beautiful Queen, I'm here for you and will never leave your side. God is in the midst of your relationship and HE is our guide. We will have ups and downs but just as God promised in HIS Word He Will be our refuge and fight our battles as long as we stay committed to HIM, for we are blessed and highly favored...For I know that many have hurt you in the past but I'm not that guy.

For I was sent to help mend your heart and place the
broken pieces back together again.

She says: Now I understand and see what it means for
God to be a part of this unity. I was still and allowed
God to speak and we are happily married and able to
speak and give our testimony for others who seek what
we now know and are glad to preach.

RUSSIAN ROULETTE

You're taken

I'm taken

We're playing Russian Roulette, what a very

Dangerous game.

My feelings for you grow each and every day. We talk,
we

laugh, you are always able to put a smile on my face, and

honestly I can't go a day without mentioning your name.

BEEN THERE

I've been there and done that but you say that you want
me

and that's a fact He says that he can treat me better
than

you and that the attention and love I will no longer lack

It sounds so good in fact too good to be true that
someone I

barely know claims he can love me better that you.

JEALOUSY

Jealousy is an ugly trait that looks good on no-one. And it

causes a lot of mistakes.

Don't hate on another female

Just because she's doing what you should be doing

Taking care of your man. Stop dissing all her pics and post

that she leaves, where she tags her friend who just so

happens to be your man.

If there is no trust in your relationship then I suggest you

get out of it.

You're sick, sick with a disease called

Jealousy

That can only be cured when you get rid of your

Insecurities

CRUSH

I have a crush on you, I can't explain, why. When I see you

I start to act shy.

We both have someone else but my heart tends to melts

Because I want you all to myself.

That sounds crazy and a little cruel for me to be falling for

someone like you.

YEARS AGO

Years ago I was young and naïve

And I didn't care nor did I believe that I would fall in love

and find my other half with whom I can spend the rest of

my life with and share many laughs.

I LOVE YOU

I love you and you love me too but somehow we seem to

lose focus on what we are destined to be.

We took our vows for better or worse, to be there for
each

other no matter how much it hurts.

But lately I feel like I can't talk to you because whatever I

say you don't seem amused and I know you feel some
kind

of way.

It must be the stress trying to pull us apart but little does
it

knows that we are mended at the heart and nothing will be

able to tear us apart.

SELF LOVE

Self-love, self-control: Be selfish when it comes to your
life

Because

You and you alone know what is toxic and what is not,

If that family member, bf/gf, wife/husband doesn't want
to

be there any longer open the door and release the
toxicants

so that your life can be purified.

MY LOVE IS A DRUG

If you don't love me just say the words.

Don't have me on this merry go round

Trying to guess your feelings...

My love is a DRUG and if you don't need it, I can and will

give it to someone who is feeling'

READ, SET, ACTION

Together forever is what you said;

But slowly I came to realize that I was dreaming to big

while you simply were playing a part, an actor on the big

screen.

Preparing your scene where you would break my heart
but

sorry to burst your bubble, your character was replaced
and

the actor is a beauty and I can't wait for the season
Finale

where I grab her by the hand and make her my wife.

DA 1 AND ONLY

I am who I am your acceptance is not needed.

Don't like what you see please feel free to have several

seats cause my feelings are not affected.

MIXED SIGNALS

I've got a man, yes I do.

But for some reason I find it easy to talk to you. You do the

things that my man ain't doing. Because of you, I smile and

I feel a deep connection.

No judgment is ever passed, and let me say that I'm starting

to feel a yearning inside but I value your friendship more

than your love.

TRUST ISSUES

I have some trust issues I genuinely do however that

doesn't mean that I don't love you. We have come from

bad relationships that have made us think twice. Our
hearts

were broken into tow by careless lovers who didn't have a

clue of what true love was and who to give it too.

COMMUNICATION

I obviously said something that you didn't like, however

instead of talking to me you run and post it on your

newsfeed for everyone to see. I wish I could know what it

is I said but you just go your way and leave me as if I'm

dead.

Is this relationship built on a lie? Because I truly love you

and I'm willing to try. No one is perfect especially not me.

But come on now stop acting like some of your apples

haven't fallen from the tree.

We are in this together, till death do us part, no matter

what

comes our way because we're mended at the heart. I love

you and always will so let's leave all this foolishness

behind us and call it our new will.

MY HEART

My heart was all yours and you acted like you didn't
know.

You played with my emotions, I was the puppet and you

were running the show. I would have done anything for
you

and you knew this to be true, however, you still took

advantage of me and my heart you broke into two.

HATERS

Haters going to hate,

When they see you doing good.

But you got to brush that negativity off and not let it
affect

you. I am in competition with no one but myself that's why

I keep pushing until I better myself. I will open up all

possible doors that are meant for me and leave your
hatin'

asses back eating my dust, exactly where you should be.

RELATIONSHIPS

Relationships come and then go.

When they end, people seem to lose control.

What they don't know is everything happens for a reason

and that's a fact.

So when you end a relationship, close that chapter in
your

book never to reopen it, not even to take a look.

YOU KNOW MY NAME

You know my name but you don't know my story.

When you would see me you would just ignore me.

Now it seems like you truly adore me.

With my name in your mouth but around me you are

faking.

If I need anything you are here is what you told me when

it

was just you and me and none of our friends.

Well let me just say please with the act because you're

truly

only hurting yourself.

I've got my life and you've got yours but for some reason

you worried about my life instead of yours.

TOGETHER FOREVER

They have been together for a minute and she thought
what

they had was real.

Until he got comfortable and treated her like a thrill

Her heart, she surrendered along with her body and
should

only to find out that she was a puppet and he was the

master running the show.

All the sweet gestures and words of affection went right
out

the door and left her second-guessing.

Is this my King/

Or did I settle because I refused to be lonely?

THOUGHTS

Man, thoughts of you and I in my head.

Thoughts of us getting naughty in your bed.

Can't be possible must not come true, we are both taken

seem like Déjà vu.

I'm pleasing you then you pleasing me then suddenly I

awake and my thoughts vanish, I try to fall back to sleep
to

continue the dream but apparently my thoughts will stay

that way,

Locked away in my dreams.

YOU THINK...

You think that you're a man but you're nothing but a

disgrace.

You think you're God's gift to women but man on man

what a harsh mistake.

Yes you have the looks and the body too, but don't

flatter

yourself boo boo.

DAMN

Damn, this can't be true,

I'm falling for a guy and it looks like

My fairy tale will never come true.

He's got a wife and I got my husband.

But from the first day we met I felt a sudden attraction.

So I sit and ponder on what to do.

But I just got to let time take its course and the rest is up
to

me and you.

CHEMISTRY

We've been talking for a while and the chemistry we have

is making me wild. I look in your eyes and I catch me in a

daze. I want to be with you. We have this relationship

that's going pretty well, so each day I hope and pray that

it

will stay that way.

We both have been hurt in the past, more than we care to

share, however I know tighter we can get through this, we

can mend our broken hearts that's in despair.

I'm falling in love with you, but I dare no say although I

feel in my heart that you truly feel the same.

BEAUTY WITHIN

She's a beauty she knows this to be true.

You can see the sparkle in her eyes and she damn sure

doesn't need reassurance from you.

She knows her worth and takes no discounts, but don't

think that it has always been this way, her heart was once

broken and she was ready to throw it away.

She gave up on love and thought she would never see
the

day where she would be crowned Queen and live happily

ever after with her King.

FORGIVENESS

I don't hate you...Whatever gave you that idea?

Just know that I move you.

Yea it took me a while.

But you no longer have the keys to my heart and think

back:

You should have never had them from the start. I was

blind, thought you loved me because you told me so many

times, but it took you leaving me for me to realize you

weren't worth 1 minute of my time.

So I don't hate you, don't even let that cross your mind...

I forgive you, and I appreciate your time...

CHASE

I will not keep chasing you and it's as simple as that because if you don't make time for me I will eventually fall back. Fall back to mend the pieces of my broken heart, it may take a while but I won't fall apart because that time will be sent loving me for me ard not worrying about what everyone else see me to be.

The time we shared was great while it lasted but you threw it all away, literally on the waste basket. You let go of a diamond, I am a beauty there is no denying but I got sick of your lies and the lack of quality time that I exited the so called game that you tried to play.

Save the fake tears and the sad love stories you had your chance to shine but instead you choose to dance alone. But in a relationship there is no "me" it should be "us' against the world you see.

So I got just one question, how that shit taste? We were winning as a team but now you are simply a disgrace. All

the time you had said you wanted to invest into building

an empire was just talk to get me inspired.

Well, I was inspired and all thanks to you. Inspired to
forget about you and build Shay's Empire. So welcome
and please watch your step, if you have any questions
proceed to the next doorstep and take it up with the
Kind who was man enough to pick up your slack.

YOU'VE BEEN

You've been on my mind for some time now. But I haven't

chalked up enough nerve to even ask you if you even feel

the same. My past has left a hole in my heart that got me

second guessing if it was meant for me to fall in love.

I get more then butterflies when I see your face. It's like

my

whole world stops. You are more than a name, more than

a simple chase, you will forever be in my heart and no

one in this crazy world will be able to take your place.

Let's start building a foundation because we have the

queen

and the king ready and willing to take their rightful places.

Our empire is coming soon so to all you haters take a few

steps back so you can observe the preparation.

77

THINKING BACK WE WERE MOVING TOO FAST

We were together for some time. I was Bonnie and you

Clyde. That instant connection is what made our bond

inseparable that it felt like we would be together for all

time. We started moving too fast and no one cared to

put

the brakes because we didn't think we would crash. But

we

did and chose to go our separate ways so please explain

why you acting brand new as if you never knew me.

Telling others it's a case of amnesia cause you swear up

and

down you never knew me. I'm not mad please never in a

million years, I'm happy that you found a new boo but there

was one little problem you thought the grass was greener

on the other side but you fucked up and noticed that the

grass was actually dry. Now you trying to come back to me

with a tear in your eye but it's too late baby boy because

that well has run dry and I don't know you cause your name

is no longer written in my sky.

SHARON THORNE-MENSAH

Sharon E. Thorne Mensah, who also goes by Shay Shay, is a 33 year old mother of three beautiful children, two girls and a boy. She was raised in Reston, Virginia and has had a passion for all kinds of music and reading romance novels since she was young. Sharon's inspiration as a poet came from her love of writing and from her brother, who was into music, as she was. She started writing at the age of 10. For her, writing was a way of escaping the bad moments she encountered and it was an alternative way for her to fully and honestly express what she was thinking and how she was feeling.

"Reflections of the Heart" is her first book. Her poems mirror the depths of life experiences, thoughts, and emotions within her heart and soul. This work of art is one of many books to come, because Sharon has the gift of words and loves to uplift and encourage as many people as she can.

She is a LION; you can hear her ROAR within her words. Sharon tells her readers to remember: *"Everything happens for a reason and there is a time and a season when you just have to keep the faith and keep believing."*

www.ingramcontent.com/pod-product-compliance
Lightning Source LLC
Chambersburg PA
CBHW051846040426
42447CB00006B/714